DATE DUE

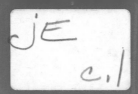

Designed and written by
Gillian Youldon and produced
by The Archon Press Ltd.
70 Old Compton Street
London W1V 5PA

The series consultant is
Henry Pluckrose, headmaster
and well-known writer and
lecturer on education.

UK edition ISBN 85166 755 4

USA edition ISBN 0-531-02389-3

USA edition Reinforced Bdg.
ISBN 0-531-00441-4

Library of Congress

Shapes

by Gillian Youldon

Franklin Watts · London · New York · Toronto · 1979

This is a circle.

How many circles can you count?

What is the new shape here?

It is a square.

Can you count the squares?

What is the new shape here?

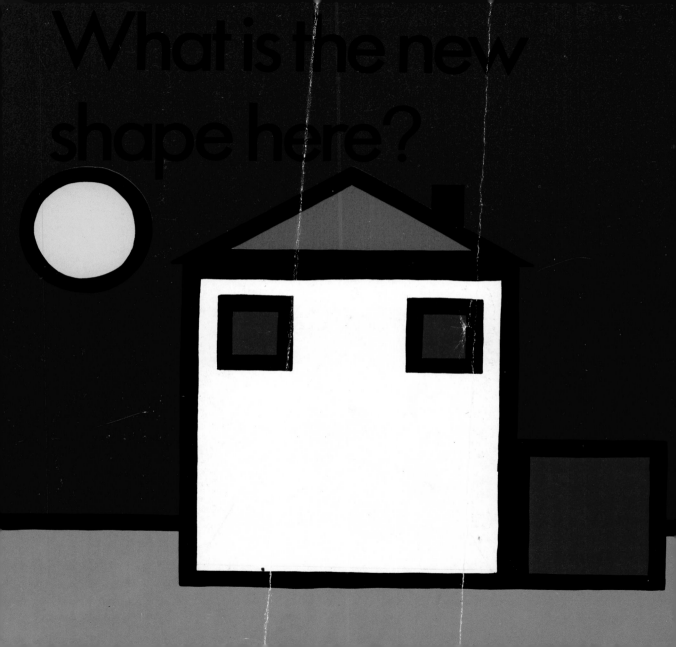

It is a triangle.

Can you count the triangles?

What is the new shape here?

It is a rectangle.

Can you count the rectangles?

What is the new shape here?

It is an
irregular shape.

Can you count the irregular shapes?

 A circle

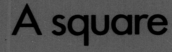 A square

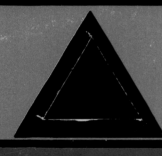 A triangle

A rectangle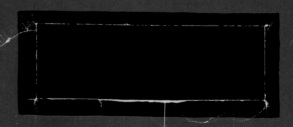

 An irregular shape